The Sand

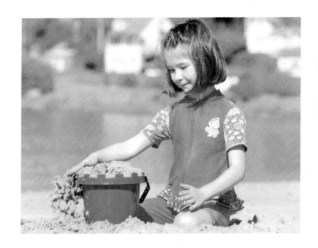

by Jane Buxton

photographs by Mark Round

Learning Media

Here is the pail.

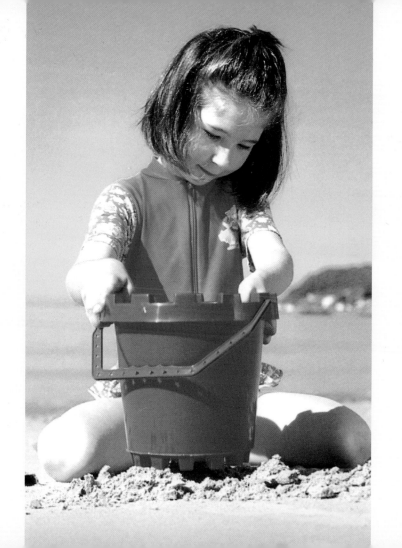

3

Here is the shovel.

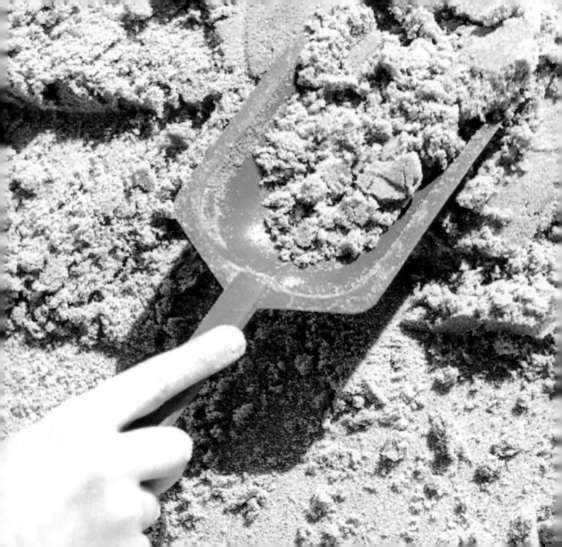

Here is the water.

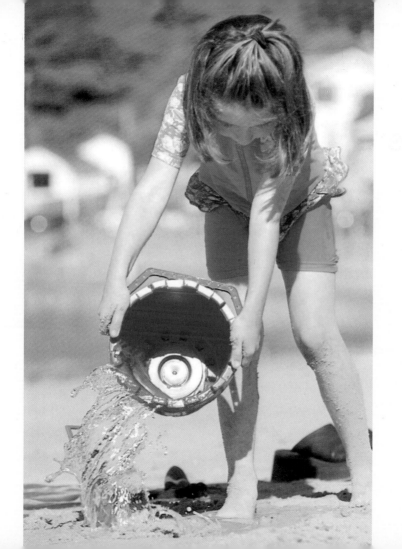

7

Here is the sand.

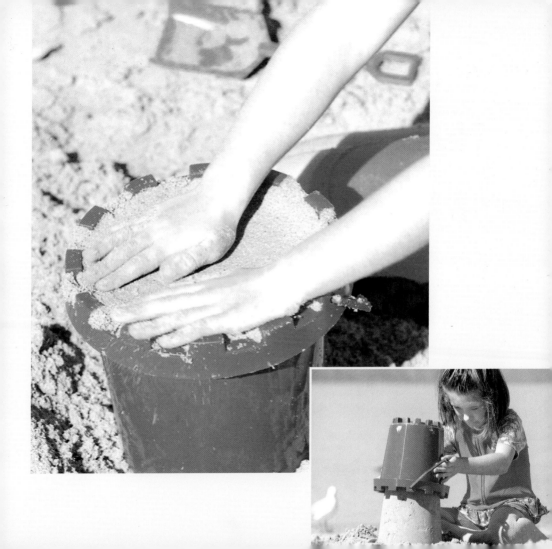

Here is the shell.

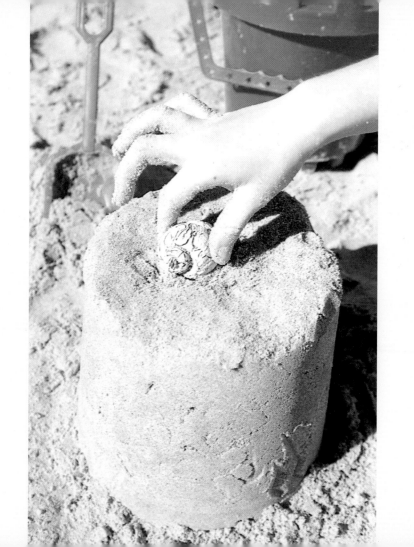

Here is the flag.

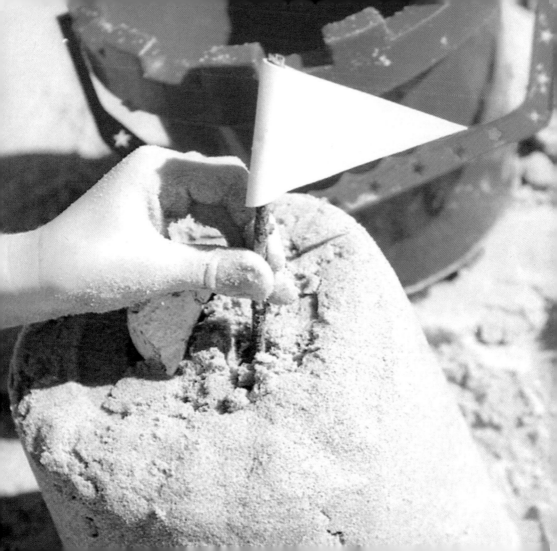

Here is the sandcastle.

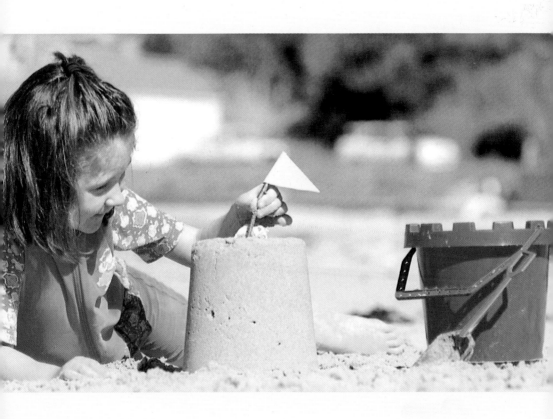

Here is the sea!

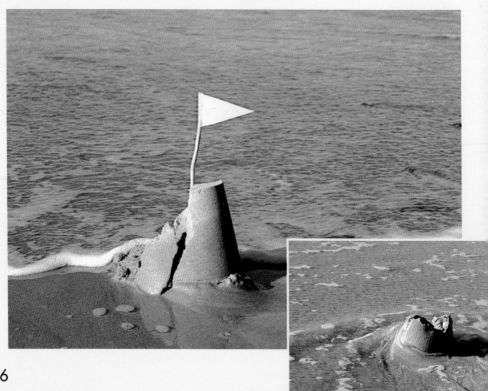